AI-POWERED CONTENT MASTERY

For Digital Marketing and SEO

By
Richard M. Powell

Disclaimer:

Table of contents

Description

Explore the ever-changing realm of content marketing by pursuing 'AI-Powered Content Mastery.' The 5Ws and H—Who, What, When, Where, Why, and How—are explored in detail in this extensive guide, which will reveal the techniques for audience analysis, relevance creating, strategic timing, ideal distribution methods, and the deep motivations that drive audience engagement. Examine the useful uses of artificial intelligence. This book provides practical tactics, real-world case studies, and a roadmap for applying AI-powered content mastery in your digital marketing and SEO initiatives, regardless of your level of experience as a marketer.

Chapter 1

Introduction

The Power of AI in Content Creation:

When it comes to producing content, artificial intelligence provides several benefits, including various chances to improve both efficiency and quality. When content creators make use of technologies that are powered by artificial intelligence, they can optimize their workflow, automate repetitive jobs, and generate more material in a shorter amount of time. AI algorithms can assist in researching, acquiring, and analyzing data, providing more accurate and comprehensive content.

Additionally, AI can aid in tailoring content to suit certain target demographics, leading to enhanced engagement and user experience. Furthermore, AI can automate activities like editing, proofreading, and translation, eliminating errors and boosting the overall quality of the text. With the benefits of AI, content creators can optimize their efforts, develop higher-quality material, and deliver it more efficiently to their consumers.

Overview of the 5Ws and H framework:
The term 5 Ws and H refers to the six essential questions to ask when gathering information or solving a problem. The questions are: 1. Who?
2. What?
3. Where?
4. When?
5. Why?
6. How?

This strategy aims to acquire a factual answer to each query. Answers to all six questions should give clarity to whatever the questioner is trying to discover: the solution to a problem, the answer to the unknown, or even the best approach to construct a product.

Chapter 2

Integrating AI for Enhanced Marketing Strategies:

In today's technology-dominated society, individuals face obstacles in reaching target audiences. However, the rise of artificial intelligence (AI) has the potential to elevate marketing methods, breaking away from the assumption that it's held primarily for huge organizations.

AI in Marketing: Definitions and Use Cases:
What is AI Marketing?

AI marketing employs data-driven analysis, natural language processing, and machine learning to give insights and automate crucial decisions, benefiting enterprises in many ways.

Use Cases:

Customer Targeting: AI refines targeting by analyzing massive data to determine preferences, habits, and demographics. This delivers insights for specific marketing initiatives focused on the proper audience.

Personalization: Facilitating experiences, AI promotes customer engagement and loyalty. Real-time data analysis provides tailored content, recommendations, and instant customer service using AI-powered chatbots.

Automation: Streamlining tasks, AI frees up time for strategic initiatives. Handling repetitive jobs boosts efficiency and minimizes expenses.

Data Analysis: AI analyzes enormous volumes of data quickly, delivering insights into customer behavior and market trends. It aids in tracking KPIs, measuring campaign effectiveness, and optimizing marketing budgets.

Customer Service: Customized chatbots boost help, prioritize requests, and give engaging thorough responses.

Advertisements: AI enhances targeting, creation, and bidding tactics, boosting efficacy and automating testing.

Email Outreach/Lead Nurture: AI automates targeted messages, saving time and resources while enhancing efficacy.

Image & Product Recognition: AI identifies things in photographs, boosting suggestions and personalizing the buying experience.

Predicting Customer Engagement: AI predicts engagement by analyzing data, including sentiments and historical encounters, aiding in strategic decision-making.

Benefits and Challenges of AI in Marketing:
Benefits: Faster decision-making, higher ROI, precise measurement of KPIs, enhanced CRM capabilities, and valuable insights from customer data contribute to adopting AI in marketing.

Challenges: Training AI systems, guaranteeing data quality, and complying with privacy rules are difficulties. Striking the correct balance is vital to prevent reputational damage and legal difficulties.

Cost is also a problem. Individuals might seek cost-effective solutions and prioritize data privacy to find a balance between personalization and honoring privacy concerns.

A Step-by-step Guide to Incorporating AI into Marketing:
1. Establish Goals: Define goals and define meaningful KPIs for AI integration based on past campaign assessments.

2. Acquire the Right Talent: Hire data scientists or consider third-party providers for AI expertise, assuring successful deployment.

3. Adhere to Data Privacy Laws: Prioritize consumer data protection and privacy to prevent legal difficulties throughout AI training.

4. Test the Quality of Data: Ensure accuracy to maximize the usefulness of AI solutions in accomplishing marketing goals.

5. Choose the Right Solution: Select an AI platform that corresponds with goals, talent, and quality data, assuring seamless integration.

Chapter 3

The 5Ws and H: Who, What, When, Where, Why and How as regards to content marketing:

It's no secret that content marketing efficiently promotes brand awareness, drives sales, and increases engagement with your target audience.

But with more marketers coming on the content marketing train each year, how can you stay competitive?

The key is in the quality of your content, not the quantity.

A successful Content Strategy offers a wonderful opportunity for brands to create a rapport with their target audience and enhance customer interaction on their digital platform. By giving relevant and valuable information to the audience businesses may strengthen their reputation and establish a community of their consumers which helps them increase brand loyalty which in turn is incredibly helpful for any business.

Creating a strong content strategy comes with loads of benefits, saving time and money, keeping the work process more structured, helping you maintain consistency in your interactions with your audience, and so on and so forth. The content strategy however does not mean only developing and delivering information on a platform. It is the complete process and method that allows businesses to attract and interact with their target audience to finally develop profitable relations with them.

A properly designed and effective content strategy must consist of 4 basic parts to be successful:

Proposition:

Your content has to add value to the life of your audience, it should stand out and the reader should have something to take away from it. Otherwise, it is quite difficult to maintain room in the reader's memory.

Strategic Planning:

You should first determine the audience you want to reach and how you can give the right content for the right audience while striking a balance with the brand requirements. Most importantly, you must have a good approach to reach the desired goal.

Brand Positioning:

Identify the brand's unique personality and attributes and find answers to how you intend the brand to be seen by the target audience. Again, define what makes the brand different and better from other competitors.

Business Care:

Understand the final aim of your content agenda and what it is that you intend to achieve with the content strategy. Also, understand how the content strategy will assist the firm's expansion.

Once you identify and grasp the 4 essential parts of establishing a solid content strategy it becomes extremely easy to create rich and enriching material that will undoubtedly break the ice between you and your audience.

Now that we know about the essential aspects and principles that need to be taken care of, here is how you can make a positive influence on your customers and guarantee that your content is engaging enough for the audience to come back for more.

What Are the 5 W's and H?

The 5 W's and H are the important questions you should ask yourself if you want to generate content that your audience would appreciate. The questions are: who, what, when, where, why, and how. By answering these questions, you better understand your audience and what they want to generate content that gives true value.

Once you learn to create value for your audience regularly, you'll keep them coming back.

These six questions are a strong tool you can utilize in all elements of your marketing plan, from blog posts and videos to your email campaigns and website architecture.

Who, what, when, where, why, and how are the answers to the five W's and the H. via use of Content Marketing

1. Who is your target market? This is the first question.

The who question is the first one to be asked since it is the most important part of your content marketing strategy; it serves as the foundation around which everything else is constructed.

The question "Who am I creating this for?" is among the most essential things to be aware of.

Who is going to get knowledge from this content?

To which segment of my target market am I directing my attention?

Because different people have different needs and interests, there is no such thing as a single product that can satisfy all of their requirements and interests. If you take a look at the market for smartphones, you will see that there are a great number of different brand names available. There are some people who are passionate about Apple, some who are enthusiastic about Samsung, and yet others who are enthusiastic about Huawei. Each of these firms generates content differently from one another so that they can be relevant to their unique client base.

This is the reason why you need to define exactly who your target market is. The one whose problem your content and product can address. The more facts you can know about these folks, the more successful your material will be. What you should do is perform a detailed study on what your clients demand, what motivates them, what information they need to make a purchase choice, etc. These questions are the building components of the people that you will need to target.

On top of establishing your target client, another set of folks that you should identify as well is who is not your target customer. You can't generate content that targets two or more different wants at the same time. Those who attempt to obtain information on the iPhone will find everything discussing Samsung rather useless and will merely bounce (and vice versa). So, establish your target customer, then build your content to fulfill the demands of this group. Then, identify those who are not the appropriate match and make sure that your material has nothing to do with this collection of people

To understand your target market better, establish a standard buyer persona for your average consumer, and spend time to explain their interests, behaviors, and routines.

If you don't know enough to develop a character, there are several methods you may gather more about your clients, including:

Surveys - Use surveys to collect client feedback.

Interviews – Chat with customers to learn more about their interests and purchase behavior.

Help desk conversations - Review your customer service requests or support tickets to discover what types of questions your customers ask and where they need help.

If you haven't begun employing information-gathering tools, it's not too late to integrate them in your website and customer interactions.

Besides defining who will profit from your content, you need to pick who will generate the stuff. That is your internal stakeholder.

Based on your understanding of client demands and habits, who has the talent and aptitude to generate high-quality content efficiently?

It may be more beneficial for small companies without a vast marketing crew to outsource content production to an expert freelancer. It all depends on your team's skills to turn around material.

2. The Second W: What Is Your Target Market Looking For?

It's sort of tough to ascertain what your target market wants, but it's pretty straightforward to establish what your audience is not disinterested in. The rationale is the purchasers are not interested in why your product or brand is fantastic; they don't care. Although you might feel the temptation to brag about why you are fantastic as a company, this is exactly the sort of stuff that clients find the least enjoyable to read.

At the end of the day, customers don't care about your brands or our brands either, customers care about the problems that they need to address. So, the message is don't write about yourself in your material if you want to attract people.

Next up, what you can do to find out about what your buyers are wanting is by doing research on keywords and search queries. When it comes to content marketing, search engines are one of the most significant tools that you need to make full use of.

Why? Search engine queries are how your audience reveals their challenges. What your audience does with search queries is just equivalent to what you and I do; when we don't know something, we google it to gain relevant information and get informed. To execute content marketing successfully, you need to comprehend the notion that most content marketing is about what your target audience is searching for on the web. If your stuff is not related with what your audience is seeking, you will be irrelevant to your consumer.

I will not cover in full what tool you may use to perform keyword research, but let me list a few of my favorites here so that you may do extra study; they are Google Keywords Planner, BuzzSumo, Ahrefts, and Semrush.

3. The Third W: When

Now that you know who you're working for and what form your material will take, it's important to determine a timeline.

This issue requires you to figure out at what time of day/week/month, you should publish your stuff (blog articles, social media updates, and so on). First, ask yourself how long it will take to generate the material and what's an acceptable timeframe for getting it done.

Then, to aid in setting priority, examine how the publication time affects your customer's value.

Is this problem urgent for your audience? Is there seasonality involved? When does your audience demand the solution?

This component is unique for your audience base; for example, if you discover that your content has the best chance to be seen when you post early in the morning but not during office time, then early in the morning is when you should publish your material.

Some forms of information are only helpful if they're delivered on time, while others might be more evergreen. Examples of seasonal information include back-to-school buying recommendations, Christmas recipes, and tax education.

One key component of the when question you need to bear in mind is you need to post consistently. You should attempt to achieve the finest quality for your content and offer values in every post and to accomplish this, you may employ IvoryResearch writing service, but you need to do it within a regular publishing schedule. This will help your consumers to know what to anticipate from you, and when you post consistently, you will have a larger chance of being remembered by your clients since they see you continually day by day, week by week, and month by month. Also, if you don't post consistently, you will be surpassed by other businesses that do so.

4. The Fourth W: Where Should You Publish And Promote Your Content?

In addition to selecting what sort of stuff to generate, you'll need to decide where to share it.

In technical words, what's the optimal marketing channel for your target audience?

You want to provide your content on the platforms that garner the maximum engagement. That's why it's vital to understand your audience's behaviors and habits in the first question.

Years ago, before the introduction of social media, answering this question was very clear as blogging was the favorite technique of gathering information. But now, this is no longer a simple question. I don't mean that blogging has gone old; it is still very alive and well and popular, but the growth of social media brings a ton of diverse platforms (Facebook, Twitter, Snapchat, Instagram, TikTok, etc.) that are all functioning on the market at the same time. As a result, the attention of the public has become scattered all over numerous platforms.

With this many outlets to select from, it looks a little bit daunting to pick where you should publish your work. However, it's not that tough in reality and the question that you need to answer properly boils down to where your prospective clientele hangs out on the web.

What does this mean? This indicates if your target customer is business people, the first site that you should focus on is LinkedIn because that is where professionals hang out. If your material involves plenty of visuals, then Instagram is the go-to destination.

All content marketers need to do is find out where the emphasis of their audience is, and then generate content that suits the environment of that platform.

For example, LinkedIn is appropriate for long-form information such as in-depth essays that break down complex concepts, whereas Facebook and Instagram embrace short-form content more.

Also, Email marketing newsletters are a superb technique to providing excellent stuff to your existing clients and subscribers. Plus, drag-and-drop email builders make it easy for you to produce attractive newsletters for all sorts of information, including video.

You may also automate emails so that clients receive them at precisely the perfect timing. If you provide software or SaaS solutions, you can leverage email automation to greet new clients and distribute training videos quickly after they sign up.

Reviewing your internal goals for the material could help you pick your channel too. For example, if your aim is greater interaction and your KPIs are likes and shares, you should distribute your work on social media.

5. The Fifth W: Why Are Your Customers Looking For Those Things?

After you have established the where, you need to carry on to figure out the why. If your audience is seeking for certain things, then why are they doing so? What problems are they encountering that make them run these search queries?

Also, you need to figure out - Why does this thing important to you?

Start by ensuring that every piece of material you post has a defined aim. Ultimately, your content strategy should correlate with your whole marketing goals and business model.

Then, assess your consumer and see if you can answer the question, "Why does my customer want this content?" What's the larger picture?

Maybe your customer wants to enhance their business by extending their customer base or strengthening their marketing approach.

Or, your customer might have more realistic results-driven goals such as boosting internet traffic or generating income.

6. The H Question: How Do You Solve Your Customer's Problem or Provide Them Value?

When you have identified the who, the what, when, where, and the why, you will need to find out about the how. The way is how you may provide your consumers value and build up relationships with them. We all don't read material for the purpose of reading, we read to solve our issues, and we want the stuff we read to solve our problems; you, your clients, or myself is no different.

So, regardless of whatever topic you're writing about, keep in mind that the number one aim of content marketing is to provide your clients value by helping them solve the problem that they want to address.

Guide for brainstorming your content using the 5 Ws and H:

The following is a list of W & H questions that you may ask yourself while you're producing your content and steer it depending on your chosen purpose.

The Who question: Who is affected?
Who is involved?
Who will benefit?
Who has this problem?

The What question: What do you need to address in this topic?
What is the key point?
What effect do you want this article to create?

The When question: When should you distribute this content to reach as many folks as possible?

The Where question: Where should you disseminate this material to reach as many people as possible?

The Why question: Why is this issue vital to your audience? Why does it matter?

Why does your audience suffer from this problem?

The How question: How to remedy the issue that you're going to address in this article?

How can you assist your consumer handle their problem?

Final Thoughts: Mastering the 5 W's (and H) for Killer Content Marketing

Let's face it. When it comes to content production, the possibilities are endless. Without a defined methodology, it's easy to feel like you're taking a shot in the dark every time you attempt to figure out what sort of content to generate next.

Delivering the greatest answers begins with asking the right questions.

The 5 W's of marketing aid in establishing a picture of your audience and how your content creates value for them. The questions might help you examine your company objectives.

All of this information enables you narrow down your alternatives until you have an effective strategy that provides value for your consumers and your firm.

In conclusion

To accomplish the final aim of establishing a respectable and efficient content strategy, finer parts should be analyzed and given appropriate weight. Building a strong brand identity via content helps companies create a relationship with their consumers and keep them coming back for more which enhances brand loyalty. Building a connection with the target audience, overcoming the language barrier, and keeping consumers engaged are a few difficulties businesses confront that may be addressed effectively with a well-planned content strategy in place.

Chapter 4

Crafting Compelling Content with Precision:

In the enormous digital expanse where content is analogous to a global language, the effort of developing something that not only draws attention

26

but also resonates is immense. Content is ubiquitous, but not all of it hits the mark. So, what distinguishes material that's swiped past, from content that leads a reader to stop, engage, and interact? This isn't merely an issue of quality, but also of relevance, connection, and the innate potential to strike a chord with the target audience.

In this extensive book, we will discuss the art and science of developing content that connects, delves deep into the psychology of the audience, meets their demands, solves their issues, and triggers an emotional reaction. This isn't about generic content but personalized tales that are written with truth, keeping with both the brand's voice and the audience's expectations.

1. Understanding the Audience: In-depth Research

Creating Buyer Personas

From the combined data, detailed buyer personas arise. These are not merely profiles but entire drawings of possible customers – replete with names, histories, concerns, and wants. Every content piece is then updated for these personas, ensuring that it is highly tailored and exactly targets specific demands and trouble spots.

Emotional Connection

Beyond the statistics and analytics, the lifeblood of content that resonates resides in the emotional connection. It's about recognizing the tiny nuances, the unstated wishes, and the quiet ambitions of the audience. Content that resonates isn't simply read; it is felt, and to generate such a reaction, the emotional factor is crucial.

Tailoring the Content: Tone and Voice

Adapting the tone and voice of the material to suit that of the audience is a critical step. It's about speaking their language, echoing their beliefs, and connecting with their ideals. This alignment develops a bond that crosses the digital gap, making the material more relevant and engaging.

Relevant and Valuable Information

Content that resonates isn't simply well-written; it is rich in value. Every word, phrase, and paragraph is supposed to deliver value, give answers, and offer solutions. It's not about the brand but the audience – reacting to their worries, addressing their issues, and expanding their knowledge.

Storytelling
Narratives have the capacity to fascinate, and when material is interwoven into compelling tales, it not only informs but also entertains and engages. Storytelling infuses material with a soul, making it more memorable, shareable, and effective.

2. Crafting Visually Appealing Content: The Power of Visuals

In the era of falling attention spans, visual material has emerged as the critical factor that not only catches but retains attention. But it's not just about adding random photographs or videos; it's about combining visuals that match, enrich, and elevate the textual information.

Customization is Key
Stock pictures, although freely accessible, may often dilute the individual touch. Custom visuals, drawings, infographics, and videos adapted to the content's context and the audience's preferences provide uniqueness and improved engagement.

Interactive Elements

Interactive content like quizzes, polls, and calculators engage the audience, making them active participants rather than passive consumers. These factors not only improve engagement but give essential information about the audience's preferences and activities.

3. SEO Alignment

Keyword Integration
While the essence of information lies in its quality and usefulness, exposure is equally crucial. SEO alignment assures that the information reaches the audience. Integrating relevant, high-search-volume keywords assures that the information is discoverable and accessible.

Quality Backlinks: amazing content generates wonderful backlinks. It's a cycle of credibility that not only enhances SEO rankings but also builds the brand's authority. The stuff that resonates is link-worthy, gaining organic backlinks that improve exposure.

Mobile Optimization

With the proliferation of mobile devices, information that is optimized for mobile viewing provides enhanced reach and accessibility. The format, style, and layout conform to the tiny screen, offering a smooth and fascinating user experience.

4. Content Amplification: Social Media Engagement

Social media isn't merely a platform for exchanging content but a tremendous instrument for amplification. Tailoring content for multiple social platforms, employing hashtags, and participating in social listening ensures that information reaches, engages, and resonates with a broader audience.

Influencer Collaborations

Collaborating with influencers that match with the brand's values helps enhance content reach. Influencers' endorsements not only boost reach but also give validity, enhancing the content's influence.

Email Marketing

Personalized email marketing may transform content into conversations. Segmented email lists, customized content, and personalized messaging guarantee that material reaches the appropriate audience, in the right format, at the right time.

5. Measuring Success: Analytics

Content that resonates is also content that performs. Analytics give insights into content performance - views, engagement, shares, and conversions. These data points aren't just numbers but essential insights that inform content strategy, ensuring it is dynamic, adaptable, and always developing.

Feedback and Engagement
Comments, shares, likes, and direct feedback are goldmines of information. They not only analyze content engagement but also give real-time feedback, allowing for content optimization and customization.

ROI Measurement
The ultimate measure of content's success lays in the ROI. It's not just about engagement but conversions. Tracking the customer's journey, from content engagement to conversion, provides insights into content's effectiveness in delivering business goals.

- **Advanced Strategies: From Content Creation to Conversion**

1. User-Generated Content (UGC)

In an era where authenticity triumphs over manicured perfection, UGC stands as a pillar of true, raw, and unedited engagement. It's the voice of the customer mirroring the brand's message.

Harnessing UGC

Brands need not only to rely on their content generation engines. Customers, the actual brand ambassadors, contribute a profusion of content daily. Encouraging, curating, and promoting UGC can improve credibility and augment the brand's content library.

Balancing Act

But with UGC comes the challenge of ensuring quality and consistency. It's about weaving these raw, different content pieces into the brand's narrative effortlessly, assuring coherence and harmony.

2. AI and Personalization: The AI Revolution

AI is currently the future; it's the present. In content marketing, AI is making personalization not just viable but scalable. Content may now be tailored to individual preferences, habits, and interactions.

Data-Driven Insights

AI algorithms trawl through massive data, obtaining appropriate findings. Each piece of content, each subject, and each style is supported by analytics, assuring that it connects with the audience not by mere coincidence, but by design.

3. Optimizing for Voice Search: The Vocal Revolution

As voice assistants infiltrate homes, voice search optimization is not optional but crucial. Content must be adjusted to the conversational, informal, and query-based character of voice searches.

4. The SEO Shift

Traditional SEO, although still vital, is developing to include voice SEO. It's about optimizing for phrases, queries, and long-tail keywords, ensuring that information is not just visible but audible.

5. Future-Proofing Content Marketing: Agile Content Strategy

In a digital world defined by flux, adaptability is the cornerstone of a successful content strategy. It's not just about reacting to trends but forecasting them, ensuring content is constantly a step ahead.

Continuous Learning

Each content piece is a chance to learn, adapt, and optimize. Analytics, feedback, and performance indicators should not merely be watched but evaluated, translating data into actionable insights for continual development.

Chapter 5

Case studies :Real-world Applications:

As the digital world continues to evolve, AI-powered digital marketing approaches are becoming more popular among enterprises. From enhancing customer experiences to growing revenue, the advantages of AI are clear. In this section, we'll take a look at some of the most inspirational AI-powered digital marketing success stories.

1. IBM Watson

IBM Watson is a robust AI platform that has been making waves in the digital marketing field. It has the capacity to analyze large volumes of data and give insights that can help organizations boost their marketing approaches. One success example comes from an airline operator that utilized IBM Watson to evaluate customer data and adjust its email marketing campaigns. The result? A substantial jump in open rates and click-through rates.

2. Coca-Cola

Coca-Cola is another firm that has effectively used AI into its digital marketing strategy. It has deployed AI to analyze client data and deliver tailored experiences for its clients. One example of this is the company's "Share a Coke" marketing, which deployed AI to make customized labels for consumers based on their names.

3. Netflix

Netflix, the world's biggest streaming service, has been in the forefront of using AI to enhance its recommendation system. By analyzing user data, Netflix was able to get insights into what content its users enjoy, and as a consequence, deliver tailored recommendations that are aligned to customers' interests and preferences. This innovative strategy not only enhanced customer satisfaction and retention but also boosted revenue growth by more than 20%. Netflix's success story is a testimony to the revolutionary potential of applying AI to generate commercial results. As organizations increasingly aim to exploit the potential of AI, it is vital to learn from the best practices of industry giants like Netflix.

4. Sephora

Sephora is a cosmetics firm that has embraced AI to improve its user experience. It has designed a chatbot that utilizes AI to give tailored suggestions and advice to its users. The chatbot is accessible 24/7, providing customers with a smooth and straightforward experience.

5. Mastercard

Mastercard is a firm that has applied AI to enhance its fraud detection ability. It leverages AI algorithms to review customer data and detect fraudulent transactions. The result is a more secure payment mechanism that provides customers piece of mind.

6. Mercedes-Benz

Mercedes-Benz is a firm that has deployed AI to deliver a tailored shopping experience for its clients. It has built an AI-powered chatbot that helps users find the ideal automobile based on their requirements and preferences. The chatbot gives individualized suggestions and assists users during the whole purchasing experience.

7. American Express

One of the greatest financial services organizations in the world has recently achieved remarkable achievements in leveraging the potential of AI to produce revolutionary consequences. Through in-depth analysis of its huge customer data, the firm was able to find crucial categories that were driving revenue growth, generating critical insights into the behaviors, preferences, and spending patterns of these client groups. This data has helped American Express to adapt its offerings and design targeted marketing efforts, resulting in better consumer engagement and retention. By embracing the newest AI technology, American Express has made a huge milestone toward attaining its mission of offering the best possible client experience, boosting its bottom line, and preserving its position as a leader in the financial services sector.

8. Starbucks

The global coffee giant is leading the way with revolutionary business methods that leverage AI to achieve disruptive consequences. By integrating AI, it has been able to improve its supply chain and eliminate waste, resulting in millions of dollars in savings every year. This was done by employing data analytics to detect trends in customer preferences, leading to more precise inventory management. Starbucks has implemented AI to boost order fulfillment, lowering wait times and enhancing the overall customer experience. Through these imaginative and forward-thinking activities, Starbucks has firmly established itself as a leader in the competitive coffee business. Their accomplishment serves as an encouragement to organizations throughout the globe to examine the capacity of AI to produce disruptive results.

9. Amazon

Amazon stands out as a superb example of a firm that has effectively deployed AI to identify purchase habits and give tailored advice to its consumers. This has resulted in more income and better client loyalty. With AI technology, Amazon is now able to monitor real-time data to keep track of which goods are selling, discover trends, and make appropriate modifications to maintain optimal performance. The company's concentration on AI has been one of the key components that have made it one of the largest e-commerce corporations in the world today.

These real-world examples illustrate that AI is not only a terrific tool for business success but also a necessary one in today's data-driven economy.

The success examples mentioned here highlight the potential of AI to deliver disruptive consequences across many businesses and topics. Organizations that have adopted these technologies are claiming large gains in productivity, efficiency, and customer satisfaction, leading to increased revenue and growth. Whether it's healthcare, banking, manufacturing, or retail, AI is proving to be a crucial tool for organizations trying to improve their operations and compete in a fast changing market. As more and more organizations strive to utilize the potential of these technologies, it's vital to keep up-to-date with the newest breakthroughs and trends to remain relevant and innovative. By adopting these groundbreaking technologies, we may build the route for a more intelligent, efficient, and prosperous future.

Chapter 6

Emerging Technologies and Their Impact:

1. Voice Search and Virtual Assistants

Voice search is altering the digital world by enabling hands-free access to information. It began in the 2010s, propelled by improvements in voice recognition and natural language processing. Now, it's a popular feature in products like smartphones and smart speakers, delivering ease and speed. Voice search translates spoken words into text and is widely applied for different tasks.

Its applications are growing, including voice commerce, healthcare, accessibility, and customer support. Industry giants like Google Assistant, Siri, Cortana, and Bixby have incorporated voice search into their platforms. This technology is transforming how we interface with information and technology, and its potential for more innovation makes it an important trend to monitor.

SEO for Voice Search: Navigating the Future of Digital Discovery

Voice search is altering the way we discover information online. Instead of typing questions, users are increasingly speaking on their devices, which has major ramifications for SEO. SEO for voice search requires altering how people speak and ask questions. For example, instead of typing "best Italian restaurants," a user may say, "What are the best Italian restaurants near me?"

Several important aspects fuel the development of voice search:

Proliferation of Voice-Activated Devices: The increased use of smartphones, smart speakers, and virtual assistants (e.g., Siri, Google Assistant, and Alexa) has made voice search more accessible and easy for consumers.

Conversational Nature: Voice inquiries tend to be more conversational and long-tail, matching how people naturally talk. Optimizing for voice search helps firms to match with these user habits.

Local Search: A major part of voice searches is location-based. Businesses that optimize for voice search could attract local consumers actively seeking for goods or services.

Competitive Advantage: As voice search gathers momentum, firms that proactively enhance their online presence may gain a competitive advantage.

To achieve this, SEO experts need to understand user intent, natural language processing, and schema markup and make sure their websites work properly on mobile devices.

Businesses that have optimized for voice search have gained success. For instance, Pizza Hut makes it simple for consumers to order using voice commands, while American Express lets users check their accounts using their voice. Domino's Pizza lets consumers order voice commands using Alexa and Google Assistant.

Voice search isn't a future notion; it's happening today. Businesses focusing on voice search optimization may better communicate with their consumers, enhance user experiences, and remain competitive online. It's about being discovered in the era of voice search.

Unlocking Marketing Opportunities with Voice Search:

Here's an overview of digital marketing themes that offer substantial promise for adopting and profiting from optimizing for voice search.

- Local Search Dominance

Many voice searches are location-based, hence optimizing for local search is crucial. This requires updating correct Google My Business listings and delivering mobile-friendly websites. An example is a small restaurant in New York City that boosted bookings and takeaway orders using voice search optimization.

- Content Strategy

Creating material that answers requests and caters to user intent is crucial for voice search. Focus on being succinct, informative, and simple to understand. Frequently asked questions (FAQ) sites, how-to guides, and material addressing common inquiries fare well in voice searches. A home improvement business, for instance, achieved success using "how-to" information. Their videos did well in voice search results, helping them position themselves as an expert.

- Conversational Marketing

Businesses may increase user experience and customer service by implementing chatbots and virtual assistants. These conversational bots can offer speedy replies to voice queries on websites, apps, or social media platforms. For example, an ecommerce business boosted engagement and conversion rates using a chatbot.

- Long-Tail Keywords

Voice search often incorporates long-tail keywords and question-based questions. Businesses may discover and target these conversational keywords to enhance visibility in voice search results. A travel business, for example, obtained higher traffic by responding specialized voice searches regarding family-friendly vacation regions.

Overall, voice search is a major marketing potential. By optimizing for local search, upgrading content strategy, adopting conversational marketing, and targeting long-tail keywords, companies may gain a competitive advantage and communicate more effectively with their audience in the era of voice search.

2. Augmented Reality (AR) and Virtual Reality (VR)

Augmented Reality (AR) and Virtual Reality (VR) revolutionize how we access digital information. These technologies generate immersive, three-dimensional experiences that make data and information come alive. AR can overlay real-time data and graphics over the actual environment, while VR delivers immersive digital surroundings.

Impact on Marketing

In marketing, AR and VR are altering how businesses connect with their consumers. AR delivers dynamic, location-based experiences via smartphone applications, enabling consumers engage with goods and services in their local surroundings.

For example, furniture businesses enable consumers to visualize how a piece of furniture might appear in their homes using AR. On the other side, VR moves customers to totally virtual situations, allowing them to experience items or services firsthand.

This includes virtual showrooms, interactive product presentations, and even virtual events. For instance, a well-known vehicle business built a VR showroom where prospective customers could examine their newest car models, customize features, and take virtual test drives. This interactive interface greatly enhanced customer engagement and purchase choices.

Impact on Businesses

AR and VR are not merely enhancing marketing efforts but also affecting whole corporate processes. These technologies are transforming remote collaboration and training. VR is being utilized for employee onboarding, safety training, and simulations. AR is employed in maintenance and repair, offering technicians real-time visual advise via smart glasses, minimizing mistakes, and boosting efficiency.

For example, large airlines may soon use AR glasses for aircraft maintenance, enabling personnel to read repair manuals, view equipment schematics, and get remote help from experts. This will simplify maintenance operations and decrease aircraft downtime.

Enhancing Customer Experiences

The most important influence is on consumers and their experiences. AR and VR are increasing consumer contact and immersion in ways previously unthinkable. From gaming to ecommerce from education to healthcare, these technologies are transforming the consumer experience.

Online garment companies such as ASOS, Zara, and Gap have incorporated an AR "try before you buy" capability, enabling buyers try on items using their telephones electronically. This decreases the uncertainty of online transactions and enhances customer satisfaction.

In short, AR and VR are disruptive technologies that are transforming digital information, revamping marketing approaches, redefining company processes, and increasing consumer experiences. As these technologies develop and become more available, their effect across sectors will only grow. Embracing AR and VR is no longer a matter of if but when for firms attempting to remain competitive in a competitive sector.

3. Interactive Advertising

Traditional advertising, defined by static graphics and one-way communication, has given place to a more dynamic and engaging strategy in the digital age. Interactive advertising immediately responds to evolving consumer expectations, wanting tailored and engaging brand experiences.

AR and VR technologies are at the front line of this shift, enabling brands to build immersive and interactive advertising campaigns that blur the barriers between the physical and digital worlds.

Interactive Advertising Through AR

This includes "try before you buy" clothing experiences, enhanced print ads with digital content, and location-specific marketing employing AR. For instance, Sephora's AR app allows customers to test different beauty items using their smartphone's camera.

Real-World Examples and Ongoing Evolution
Companies like IKEA, Lowe's, and Nissan leverage AR and VR for immersive customer experiences, from picturing furniture at home to planning kitchens and conducting virtual test drives. Interactive advertising is not just a passing novelty but represents increasing customer expectations.

As AR and VR technology evolves, we can anticipate ever more compelling advertising experiences that alter how brands communicate with their audiences in the digital age.

AR in ECommerce
AR bridges the gap between in-store experiences and the virtual world. It promotes product visualization by letting consumers engage with virtual copies of things in their physical surroundings. This lowers uncertainty in online

purchases and delivers compelling experiences, including customization.

Convenient Implementations of AR in ECommerce

AR provides virtual try-ons, furniture visualization, interactive product demos, and better packaging. For example, apparel firms like Converse and Warby Parker provide AR try-on capabilities, while shops like Wayfair let shoppers to imagine furniture in their homes.

Lenskart employs AR for virtual try-ons of eyeglasses and sunglasses. Target provides the "See It in Your Space" option, while Modiface interacts with cosmetic companies for rich virtual try-on experiences. Brands like Estée Lauder and MAC Cosmetics leverage Modiface's technology.

Overall, AR revolutionizes e-commerce by delivering immersive, interactive, and customized buying experiences. It provides practical applications, from virtual try-ons to interactive product demonstrations, transforming the digital retail landscape for better customer enjoyment.

4. Internet of Things (IoT) and Connected Devices

At its essence, the Internet of Things (IoT) refers to the network of physical objects or "things" that are combined with sensors, software, and connections, allowing them to gather and exchange data with other devices and systems via the Internet. These "things" may be ordinary items like thermostats, light bulbs, vehicles, and wearable technologies like fitness trackers.

Data-Driven Marketing utilizing IoT

Here's how IoT has altered data-driven marketing:

Harnessing real-time data streams: IoT devices continually capture data from different sources, offering insights into consumer behaviors and preferences.

Personalization and targeted marketing: IoT data enables marketers develop highly tailored campaigns and provide unique content, suggestions, and offers that connect with individual consumers.

Enhanced consumer engagement: IoT fosters real-time customer relations, delivering proactive solutions and generating brand loyalty.

Predictive analytics: IoT data delivers predictive analytics, allowing firms anticipate consumer expectations, optimize approaches, and make educated choices.

Location-based marketing: IoT devices with location-tracking capabilities enable for geo-targeting advertising, providing location-specific offers to clients.

Industry examples include:

Retail: Smart shelves gather data for improved product placement and inventory management.

Automotive: IoT-connected autos give data regarding driving behavior for tailored services and maintenance advice.

Healthcare: Wearable health devices transmit real-time patient data, allowing remote monitoring and prompt actions.

In conclusion, these evolving technologies provide new prospects for data-driven insights, better consumer experiences, and targeted interaction in the context of digital transformation. Embracing these innovations positions firms to succeed in a future where the digital and physical worlds are growingly interwoven, with an emphasis on customer-centricity and data-driven decision-making.

Chapter 7

Conclusion:

In conclusion, our tour through the realms of AI in content creation has proven the revolutionary potential it holds in establishing marketing approaches, creating correct material, and effecting real-world applications. As we stand at the confluence of technology and creativity, the case studies presented attest to its actual influence. The changing picture of evolving technologies further highlights the demand for adaptability. In conclusion, this investigation provides a compass for navigating the dynamic world of AI, pushing us to harness its potential for creativity and excellence in content production.